MALLARD DUCKS

Amy-Jane Beer

Grolier
an imprint of
SCHOLASTIC

www.scholastic.com/librarypublishing

Contents

Published 2008 by Grolier
An imprint of Scholastic Library Publishing
Old Sherman Turnpike, Danbury,
Connecticut 06816

© 2008 Grolier

For The Brown Reference Group plc
Project Editor: Jolyon Goddard
Copy-editors: Ann Baggaley, Lisa Hughes
Picture Researcher: Clare Newman
Designers: Jeni Child, Lynne Ross,
Sarah Williams
Managing Editor: Bridget Giles

Volume ISBN-13: 978-0-7172-6269-4
Volume ISBN-10: 0-7172-6269-3

**Library of Congress
Cataloging-in-Publication Data**

Nature's children. Set 3.
p. cm.
Includes bibliographical references and
index.
ISBN 13: 978-0-7172-8082-7
ISBN 10: 0-7172-8082-9
1. Animals--Encyclopedias, Juvenile. I.
Grolier Educational (Firm)
QL49.N384 2008
590.3--dc22
2007031568

Printed and bound in China

PICTURE CREDITS

Front Cover: **Shutterstock:** Karel Broz.

Back Cover: **Shutterstock:** Ronald
Caswell, Philip Eppard, Robert Pernell,
Michael Sexton.

Alamy: Manor Photography 42; **FLPA:**
David Hosking 38; **Nature PL:** Pete Cairns
22; **NHPA:** Joe Blossom 10, David Woodfall
46; **Photolibrary.com:** Michael Gadomski
9; **Shutterstock:** Bronwyn Photo 37, Karel
Broz 21, Ronald Caswell 41, Joseph Gareri 5,
Ronnie Howard 18, Lana Langlois 14,
Lenzshooz, Inc. 4, Steve McWilliam 26–27,
Evan Meyer 30, Robert Pernell 2–3, 17, Susan
Quinland-Stringer 34, Jeff Schultes 6, 13, Sue
Smith 33, Nancy Tripp 45, Feng Yu 29.

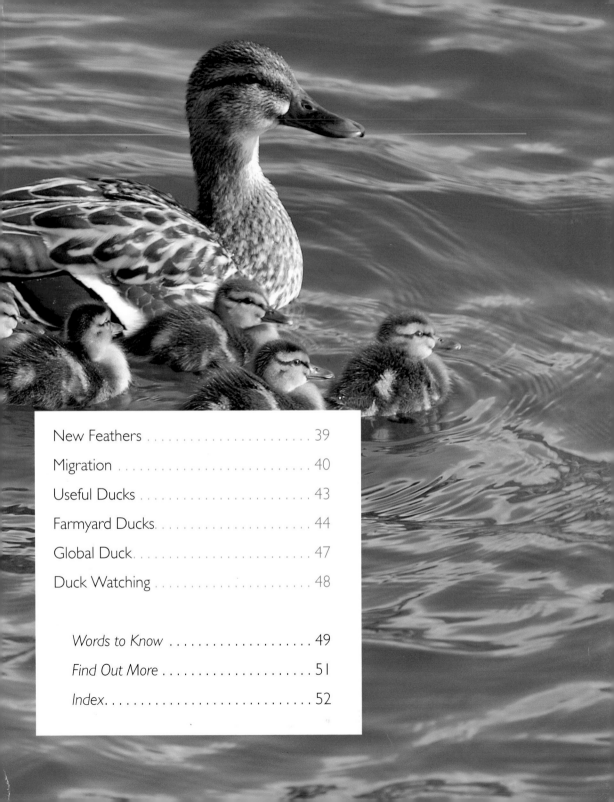

FACT FILE: Mallard Ducks

Class	Birds (Aves)
Order	Anseriformes
Family	Ducks, geese, and swans (Anatidae)
Genus	Dabbling ducks (*Anas*)
Species	Mallard (*A. platyrhynchos*)
World distribution	North America, Europe, Asia, Greenland, and North Africa; introduced by humans to Australia, New Zealand, and many islands, including Bermuda
Habitat	Rivers, lakes, and ponds in forests, woodlands, scrublands, and open county
Distinctive physical characteristics	Male is gray and dark brown with a shiny green head and white collar; female is mottled grayish brown and black
Habits	Feed by upending in water; noisy in breeding season; some northern mallard ducks fly south for winter
Diet	Plant matter, insects, and small water animals

Introduction

Mallards are the world's most well-known wild ducks. They can almost always be seen lakeside in parks, gardens, and in nature reserves. Humans tamed mallard ducks thousands of years ago. The **descendants** of those ducks are the types of ducks—usually white—that live on farms today. In fact, only one type of farmyard duck, the Muscovy duck, is not descended from the mallard. Male mallards have showy, colorful feathers and are easy to recognize. The females are duller, but this coloration serves a very good purpose: it keeps them hidden from enemies when the ducks are raising their young.

The hallmark of a male mallard is a green-blue head, yellow beak, and orange legs.

Mallards are the most
common type of duck
in the world.

In Their Element

Ducks are among those rare animals that seem to have mastered living on land, on water, and in the air. Think of all the artificial aids humans have to use to manage the same feats. Humans manage well moving about on land, but when it is cold or wet we need all kinds of different clothes to help us stay warm and dry. The duck manages with one outfit—its feathers—that lasts all season.

Few humans can swim as well as ducks. Sometimes the ducks will stay on the water for weeks at a time—humans need a boat to do that, not to mention goggles or a mask to see underwater as well as ducks do. And not only can ducks fly, they can take off from land or water—humans need two types of airplanes to achieve that!

In the Beginning

Female mallards usually lay one egg each day for one to two weeks. A group of eggs laid together is called a **clutch**. It takes about four weeks for a baby mallard to develop inside its egg. Once the clutch is complete, the mother duck starts to sit on them. By keeping the eggs in contact with her body, the mother duck warms them up. That is called incubation. The warmth makes the baby **ducklings** develop. Once the mother starts the process, she must see it through to the end. If at any time the eggs go cold, the growing chicks inside will die.

Mallards' eggs are about the same size as chickens' eggs.

9

The egg tooth, which
young birds use to
break out of their
shell, falls off a few
weeks after the
bird hatches.

Hatching Out

Every day, the devoted mother duck turns the eggs over with her beak, or bill, making sure the eggs stay warm all the way through. Sometimes she will quack quietly to them, too, until one day her calls are answered by muffled cheeps. At this time the mother duck knows her babies are ready to break out of their eggshells, or hatch. She stands protectively by as they struggle first to make a hole in the eggshell, and then to crack it all the way around.

A duckling uses a special peg on the end of its beak called an egg tooth to pierce the eggshell and weaken it. But it still takes all the duckling's strength to force the broken shell apart.

Fluffballs

Newly hatched ducklings are wet with the remains of the egg white that protected them while they were developing. If they are lucky, the Sun will be shining on the day they hatch, and they will dry out in no time.

The ducklings are covered in very soft, fluffy feathers called **down**. As the down dries, it fluffs up until the skinny duckling looks almost round. Down feathers are very important. They are slightly greasy, which makes them waterproof. The fluffy down traps a lot of air around the duckling's body. The air keeps the baby bird warm and dry and helps it float.

Mallards usually build their nest close to or on the ground. Sometimes, they use holes in trees. For mallards that nest in trees, the fluffy down also protects the ducklings from injuring themselves when they have to leave the nest and jump to the ground.

Once ducklings have hatched and followed their mother to water, they never return to the nest.

When out of the water, ducklings have to be especially careful and watch out for land predators.

Enemies Everywhere

There is a good reason why mallards have a large brood—there's a very good chance most of the ducklings will not survive. The first weeks of life are a very dangerous time for mallards as they are hunted by all kinds of **predators**. If a clutch of ten eggs all hatch, often there will only be two or three lucky ducklings left just one week later.

On land, cats, ermine, raccoons, and various snakes all enjoy a meal of duck eggs or ducklings. In water, there are dangers lurking, too, in the form of snapping turtles, toothy pikes, and other large fish.

Keep Up!

Baby mammals, such as kittens, puppies, and human infants feed on milk. Baby birds, such as ducklings, however, do not get milk and have to start eating solid food immediately. They get lessons in swimming and finding food on their very first day out of their egg. This is a dangerous time. The smartest thing a duckling can do is stay as close as possible to its mother. She will do her best to protect her young. It is usually the stragglers—the ducklings that don't keep up with their mother—that get picked off by predators.

Like other ducks and geese, ducklings form a very close bond with their mother as soon as they hatch. She is usually the first living thing they see, and they will do their best to stay by her side, wherever she goes. This bond is called **imprinting**. If the ducklings are raised by humans they can form the same kind of attachment to a person—or to any other animal they first see, such as a chicken or a dog!

Mallard ducklings are raised by their mother only.

17

Male mallards have a distinctive white collar of feathers around their neck.

18

Duck Design

Mallard ducks are large birds, measuring up to 27 inches (70 cm) long. They weigh about 3 pounds (1.3 kg). That is much less than a mammal of a similar size, but still somewhat heavy for a bird. It takes a lot of power to carry this weight in flight, and therefore mallards have very large breast muscles. Those are the muscles that flap the wings. They are also the part of the duck that other animals, including humans, like to eat.

Because they have many predators, mallard ducks have sharp senses. Their bright eyes are on the sides of their head so that they see almost all around them at once. Their sensitive ears are hidden by feathers on the sides of the head.

Webbed Feet

Ducks have very big feet. Each foot has three long toes that point forward and a short fourth toe that forms a kind of **dewclaw** at the back. The three long toes are joined with a web of tough skin. The webbing makes an excellent paddle. It also makes it easier for the duck to walk on soft mud because the webbing spreads out the duck's weight over a larger area. That stops the feet from sinking into the mud. A duck's feet work like a diver's flippers and snowshoes combined! Ducks can walk on snow, but they struggle with ice, slipping and sliding and getting very cold feet. If they have to stand on ice for very long they usually use just one foot. They tuck the other foot in the downy feathers to keep it warm, swapping the feet over every few minutes.

Mallards have
perfect balance
while standing
on one foot.

21

A male mallard
calls out across
a frozen lake.

Paddle Power

If you look at the position of a duck's legs on its body you'll see they are set very far back. That is why they waddle as they walk. They'd find moving on land easier if their legs were attached right in the middle of the body. But there is a very good reason why that is not the case. Having legs and feet set toward the back of the body makes swimming much easier. Think of a power boat—the engine and propellers are always at the back. The best bird swimmers are penguins and their legs are right at the back when they swim. It's a tricky balancing act though, as legs at the back are not very good for walking—penguins are amazing swimmers, but pretty hopeless on land. By having their legs just slightly toward the back, ducks manage to be pretty good at both walking and swimming.

Waterproofing

The feathers on a duck's body, and especially those on its back, are oily. Oil and water do not mix, so any water that touches the feathers forms little beads like those on a freshly waxed car or a brand-new waterproof coat. These droplets run straight off the feathers without soaking in. The duck can dry itself completely with just a quick shake.

Have you heard the phrase "like water off a duck's back"? People use it when they mean someone copes so easily with a situation that it doesn't seem to affect him or her at all. Think of politicians ignoring the bad things that are said about them—they seem to cast off the insults as easily as ducks shed water.

Quack Quack?

Everyone knows what a duck sounds like. It's one of the first animal noises young children learn. But did you know that the very loud, far-carrying "quack, quaaaack quack" sound so well known is only given by female mallards? The voices of male ducks, or **drakes**, are feeble by comparison. The closest thing drakes can manage to the female quack is a wheezy "whh-aab" sound.

Both males and females sometimes give other calls, including grunts, whistles, and soft muttering sounds. Ducklings can keep up an almost continuous high-pitched cheeping as they try to keep in touch with their mother while exploring their new world.

The mallard's paddlelike feet, toward the back of its body, power it through water.

Dabbling for Dinner

Ducks eat all kinds of things. They're not at all fussy, and they rarely miss a chance to try something new. Most of their food is plant matter, such as shoots, leaves, roots, and seeds. They find this food on land and in water. When you see a duck swimming with its bottom up in the air and its head under the water it is hunting for things to eat. This way of feeding is so distinctive it even has its own name: **dabbling**.

Ducks also eat food that is floating or swimming near the water's surface, such as seeds, pieces of bread, and insects; even small fish will be quickly picked up. The duck's beak has a jagged, or serrated, edge, which lets water drain from the food before it is swallowed.

Mallards can dive fully underwater to find food but prefer to upend, or dabble, when grazing on water plants.

29

A drake's head feathers are iridescent—they appear to be different shades of green and blue in the sunlight.

Dressed to Impress

Mallard drakes are extremely handsome birds, especially in the **breeding season**. A drake in his prime looks magnificent. His beak is bright yellow, and the feathers on his head are a metallic blue-green that shine splendidly in the sunlight. There is a distinctive white collar around his neck, and his breast feathers are a rich chocolate brown, often with the same metallic gleam as the head feathers. The rest of his body is soft gray, rich brown, and pitch black, with a dazzling blue flash on each of the wings. The tail is very dark green and white, with a couple of small curls. A pair of bright orange feet complete the colorful image. All these colorful parts make the mallard drake one of the easiest ducks to recognize.

Fantastic Father?

Of course mallard drakes do not go to all the trouble of growing and caring for gorgeous **plumage** just so humans can admire them. There is a much more important reason for their good looks. For drakes, perfect glossy plumage is a clear sign they are in healthy condition, and that in turn means they are probably naturally strong and not prone to disease. That makes a male attractive to female mallards, who want to have healthy ducklings and are looking for the best possible drake to father them. If a male is even slightly unhealthy, it will show in his feathers—they will look dull or patchy. Female mallards are much less likely to be interested in a shabby male.

Ducks have very good
color vision, which
enables the females
to admire a drake's
showy colors.

A drake and a female duck stay together until the female is ready to lay eggs.

34

Chasing the Girls

A female mallard can have a rather hard time during the breeding season. Drakes can make a real nuisance of themselves, following her everywhere so she barely gets a moment's peace. Furthermore, the males are not very good at respecting a female's decision once she has chosen a **mate**. Often a female will be chased down by several drakes. There is even a danger that she might be accidentally drowned as they all try and get close to her!

Dull for a Reason

Compared to drakes, female mallards appear rather dull at first glance. But close up you'll see that while the males' eye-catching outfit is made up of patches of plain colors, females have more intricate patterns. Their feathers are a gorgeous blend of dark and light brown, black, and gray, with a patch of shimmery blue on the wings.

This dull plumage has an important purpose. Under the right conditions, the earth-toned colors and delicate pattern make her almost invisible. After mating, she builds a nest among dead leaves. While she sits there perfectly still, a person could come within a few feet and never know she was there. Her perfect **camouflage** protects her and her precious eggs.

The outside of a bird's beak is made from a horny substance called keratin.

The duller feathers of drakes during winter is called eclipse plumage.

New Feathers

Over time, a mallard's feathers get frayed and worn. In order to stay in good shape for flying—and to stay warm and dry on water—the birds need to shed old feathers and grow new feathers. This process is called **molting**. In winter, the males copy the females' sensible, drab plumage. At this time, when the mating season is well past, there is no need for the drakes to impress females with their bright plumage. Staying safe from predators by having feathers that act as camouflage is much more important.

Molting can be inconvenient for ducks. At some point, they have to shed their flight feathers. That means for a few weeks while they are waiting for the new ones to grow they cannot fly. While molting flight feathers, the ducks spend most of their time out on the water, as far as possible from land predators.

Migration

In parts of North America, Europe, and Asia, life becomes impossible for mallards in winter. Rivers, lakes, and ponds freeze over and the land is covered with snow, leaving nowhere for the ducks to find food. They have no choice but to fly south in **flocks**. The ducks will stay in their southern homes until spring returns. At that time the birds head north again. These long, seasonal journeys are called **migrations**.

It almost seems more logical for the mallards to live farther south all year round, but they have a good reason for taking the trouble to fly north. In northern lands, the summer days are very long, and plants and animals grow and breed very quickly. For a few short months there is so much food that the ducks can get very fat and raise far more young than they could farther south.

During long migrations, mallards fly very high, up to 4 miles (6.5 km) above the ground.

Mallards are a
common sight
in city parks.

Useful Ducks

Because many people enjoy eating duck meat, ducks are farmed or hunted. Hunting ducks is relatively easy because they can be shot as they fly in the air or swim on water. They are then collected by specially trained dogs.

Ducks are so good at looking after themselves that they are easy to farm for their meat and eggs. (Duck farms are most common in East Asia.) As well as good meat and eggs, ducks provide another useful resource in the form of their feathers. Long ago, duck feathers were used as quills for writing. Their soft down is still used to stuff quilts, pillows, and duvets and to line winter clothing.

Many people love ducks simply because they look beautiful. For this reason ducks are often allowed to live in parks and gardens where people can come to admire and feed them.

Farmyard Ducks

If you picture a typical farmyard, or **domestic**, duck, you might imagine a big white bird with an orange beak. There are dozens of breeds of domestic ducks. Although many of them do not look much alike, most are descended from the mallard duck.

People have been breeding ducks for thousands of years. By choosing which ducks are allowed to breed together, farmers have been able to create types with special characteristics. Most farm ducks are large. Larger birds have more meat. Ducks are also bred to remain white because most people prefer quilts that are stuffed with white down.

This domestic
duck has head
feathers that look
like a bonnet.

A small flock
of mallards rests
on a frozen lake
in England.

Global Duck

Mallard ducks occur naturally in most parts of the northern hemisphere—that is the "top" part of our planet—in North America, Central America, Europe, Asia, and North Africa. With a little help from humans, mallard ducks are now also doing well in the wild in Australia and New Zealand. The mallard is now probably the world's best-known duck.

In North America, the mallard is a familiar sight in the countryside and even in big cities. They are good at spotting even very small ponds from the air and will fly down to check out small park lakes and even garden ponds and swimming pools. If they discover enough food there, they might settle for good. Life can be easy in the city for mallard ducks because people like to feed them!

Duck Watching

Anyone can watch ducks, especially in parks where they are used to people and quite tame. Trying to watch mallards in the wild is more difficult, but more rewarding. Many nature reserves have **hides**—small huts that people can sit in to watch the birds. Nestled in these hides, with a good pair of binoculars, observers can get a close up view of the birds' fine feathers!

While watching mallards, there's a good chance of seeing other types of ducks, too. Some of them look very similar to mallards, in particular the black duck. Both male and female black ducks look like mallard females, but their feathers are much darker. The blue patch on their wings doesn't have the same white border. Female black ducks have a grayish brown beak, whereas the drakes have a yellow beak.

Words to Know

Breeding season The time of year when animals come together to produce young.

Camouflage Markings that help an animal blend in with its surroundings so that it cannot be seen by predators or prey.

Clutch A group of birds' eggs.

Dabbling Feeding technique in which the duck upends itself to reach food on the bottom.

Descendants An animal's offspring.

Dewclaw A toe at the back of the foot that is not used as much as the other toes.

Domestic Raised and tamed by humans.

Down Small, soft feathers close to the skin.

Drakes Male ducks.

Ducklings	Baby ducks.
Flocks	Groups of ducks.
Hides	Shelters used by people for watching wildlife.
Imprinting	The way baby ducks fix on the first moving thing they see when they hatch, usually their mother.
Mate	Either of a breeding pair; to come together to produce young.
Migrations	Seasonal journeys made to look for food, warmer weather, mates, or a place to raise young.
Molting	Shedding old feathers so that they can be replaced by new ones.
Plumage	A bird's feathers.
Predators	Animals that hunt other animals.

Find Out More

Books

Miller, S. S. *Waterfowls: From Swans to Screamers*. Animals in Order. New York: Franklin Watts, 2001.

Zemlicka, S. *Mallard Ducks*. Pull Ahead Books. Minneapolis, Minnesota: Lerner Publications, 2004.

Web sites

Mallard Duck (Anas plathyrhynchos)
animals.nationalgeographic.com/animals/birds/
mallard-duck.html
Information about mallard ducks.

Mallard Ducks
www.enchantedlearning.com/subjects/birds/printouts/
Mallardprintout.shtml
Facts and a picture of mallard ducks to print.

Index

52